Under, Over, By the Clover

What Is a Preposition?

To Patrick, Clare, Fiona, and Luke,
who are **BEYOND** good. —B.P.C.

To the indomitable Spot
—B.G.

Preposition: A word that connects a noun or pronoun to other words in a sentence.

Under, Over, By the Clover

What Is a Preposition?

by Brian P. Cleary

illustrated by Brian Gable

🍀 CAROLRHODA BOOKS, INC. / MINNEAPOLIS

beside the chair—

under,
over,
by the
clover,

About,
above,
or next to
Rover.

They tell us

time and also place,

in
between
the pond
and pool.

Ever since the olden days,
there's been a silly myth

That **prepositions** aren't correct to end a sentence **with**.

But write your sentence carefully,
and you'll discover that

Ending
with a
preposition

is often where it's **at**.

Prepositions give direction

Like, doctors rushed
to Rhonda's Wrecked shin.

Or charlie danced
the charleston
over on the green,

Down, beyond,
around the bend,
along the old
ravine.

Across
the way,

toward
MISSISSIPPI,

Through
the yard
of Chris, the hippie.

Prepositions do their job

in a way
that just
amazes—

Go Pitt!!

Like, Paul's **from** Pittsburgh,

Way **up** there,

I hid beneath
the old oak chair—

Into, inside,
from the zoo,

Home by way of Timbuktu.

They tell the
whens, the wheres,
the hows,

'cause that's their special mission,

and help to link the other words—

that's what's a preposition!

So, what is a

Preposition?

Do you know?

ABOUT THE AUTHOR & ILLUSTRATOR

BRIAN P. CLEARY is the author of several other picture books, including <u>A Mink, a Fink, a Skating Rink: What Is a Noun?</u>, <u>To Root, to Toot, to Parachute: What Is a Verb?</u> <u>Hairy, Scary, Ordinary: What Is an Adjective?</u>, and <u>Rainbow Soup: Adventures in Poetry.</u> He lives in Cleveland, Ohio.

BRIAN GABLE lives and works in Toronto, Ontario, with his wife, Teresa, and two children, Kristin and Stephen.

This book is available in two editions:
Library binding by Carolrhoda Books, Inc., a division of Lerner Publishing Group
Soft cover by First Avenue Editions, an imprint of Lerner Publishing Group
241 First Avenue North, Minneapolis, MN 55401 U.S.A.

Website address: www.lernerbooks.com

Library of Congress Cataloging-in-Publication Data

Cleary, Brian P., 1959—
    Under, over, by the clover : what is a preposition? / by Brian P. Cleary ; illustrated by Brian Gable.
       p.   cm. — (Words are categorical)
    ISBN 1-57505-809-X (lib. bdg. : alk. paper)
1. English language—Prepositions—Juvenile literature. [1. English language—Prepositions.] I. Gable, Brian, 1949— ill. II. Title.
PE1335.C581 2002
428.2—dc21   2001001263

Manufactured in the United States of America
5 6 7 8 9 10 - JR - 09 08 07 06 05 04